I've Got a Song in Baltimore

by Matthew McCoy

Folk Songs of North America and the British Isles

SMC 574

SCHOTT

Mainz • London • Madrid • New York • Paris • Prague • Tokyo • Toronto

This book is dedicated to Doreen Falby, Christine Shuart Saunders,
Daniel LeJeune, Bradley Permenter and the children of
the Peabody Children's Chorus
for whom many of these arrangements were created.

SMC 574

ISMN 979–0–60001–052–3
UPC   8–41886–01589–0
ISBN   978–1–84761–255–7

Design, typesetting and music engraving by William Holab

Contents

INTRODUCTION

I've Got a Song in Baltimore is a collection of arrangements of folk songs from North America and the British Isles that were created during the years from 1998 through 2008. With the exception of *Great Big House in New Orleans* and *Sleep, Little One*, the arrangements were conceived as performance pieces for children's chorus with Orff instrument accompaniment and have been performed by ensembles at The Potomac School in McLean, Virginia and The National Cathedral School for Girls in Washington, D.C., as well as the Peabody Children's Chorus in Baltimore, Maryland (hence the title of this collection). In light of this distinction of purpose, many of the arrangements present thick instrumental textures that, while providing interest and complexity to the accompaniment, may overwhelm small groups of singers without some adaptation of instrumentation and/or rhythmic and melodic patterns. Additionally, a limited number of parts are appropriate for advanced students and/or other teachers to perform and as such, it is acceptable to have a large number of young singers participate with a handful of more advanced players.

It is recommended that students possess some facility with pitched and non-pitched percussion prior to learning to play these arrangements. An excellent resource for teaching and reviewing the fundamentals of technique for pitched percussion (i.e., xylophones, glockenspiels, and metallophones) is the book *Playing Together*, by Jane Frazee, also published by Schott Music Corporation. Further, the pieces in this collection have been ordered so that they progress from technically easier to more difficult.

In addition to the arrangements, this collection also includes suggestions for teaching. As is common with process-based teaching, many of the accompaniment patterns are prepared through speech and/or body percussion and then transferred to instruments at a later stage. Additionally, the sequential development of simple rhythmic and melodic patterns and phrases to more complex ones is presented where appropriate. (For further explanation regarding the teaching strategies used in this collection as well as many others, see *Pieces and Processes*, by Steven Calantropio, published by Schott Music Corporation.) In situations where a majority of students can read and perform from standard notation, much of the process may be abbreviated if not eliminated. Regardless of the processes used to teach an arrangement, the teacher is encouraged to consider the following:

- Students should be thoroughly familiar with melodies and lyrics prior to beginning work on accompaniments.

- It is highly recommended that body percussion and barred instrument parts be presented by the teacher in mirror imitation (e.g., when facing students, the teacher's right hand is visually associated with the students' left hands).

- Melodies may often be sung or performed on an instrument (e.g., soprano recorder) by the teacher as students are learning accompaniments.

- Consistent references to the formal structure of a piece may help students learn accompaniments more rapidly.

- Artistic teaching contributes greatly to musical performances; what a teacher models in the process, the students will imitate as they learn and perform.

ACKNOWLEDGEMENTS

Since the mid-1990s I have been fortunate to learn from and work alongside master teachers of Orff Schulwerk in several teacher education courses in the United States. These teachers have positively influenced my views and practices regarding music and movement education, and they continue to inspire me through their artistry and dedication to the work. It is to them that I offer heartfelt thanks for the impact they have made on my professional development over the years.

In relation to this publication, I wish to thank and acknowledge three individuals for their significant contributions to my understanding of arranging and composing works for children and Orff instruments. The first is Cindy Hall, who teaches in the Orff Schulwerk certification programs at the University of St. Thomas in St. Paul, Minnesota, and the University of Kentucky. Cindy's sage advice given at the start of my education in the Schulwerk was always to "keep it real" by considering the children for whom we compose and arrange. Through the years, I can say that her emphasis on the practical has been a guiding principle in much of my creative activity in music education. Second is Jane Frazee, former director of the Orff Schulwerk certification program at the University of St. Thomas. I was fortunate to be a student of Jane's for the orchestration and arranging component of my Level III experience and it is because of her encouragement that I considered publishing as a possibility. Finally, I wish to thank and acknowledge Steve Calantropio, currently serving as the Education Director of the American Orff-Schulwerk Association, who over the years has been my teacher, mentor, colleague, and friend. Steve is one of the finest process teachers I have ever had the benefit to observe and learn from, and his influence has resulted in much of what is contained within the pages of this publication.

I also wish to acknowledge the patience and support given to me by Carolee Stewart and Wendy Lampa over the past several years while this publication was being written, edited, and published. Without their efforts, this collection would not be as it is today.

Last, I need to thank the many students for whom these arrangements were written. Their dedication to artistic music making has always served as both inspiration and encouragement and I consider it an honor to have shared in their musical experiences through various performances of the pieces in this collection.

STEM DIRECTION IN NOTATED EXAMPLES

In some cases, the stem direction of specific notated examples indicates whether the right or left hand is to be used by the student when performing various notes in an accompaniment pattern. Where it appears that no indication of stem direction has been made, "handedness" is not crucial for performance of that particular part or pattern. Teachers are encouraged to model body percussion and instrumental technique in "mirror" imitation facing the students (i.e., student right hand = teacher left hand, student left hand = teacher right hand).

$\downarrow$ = right hand

$\uparrow$ = left hand

INSTRUMENTS AND ABBREVIATIONS

V	Voice
SR	Soprano Recorder
SG	Soprano Glockenspiel
AG	Alto Glockenspiel
SX	Soprano Xylophone
AX	Alto Xylophone
FC	Finger Cymbals
Tr.	Triangle
Cym.	Suspended Cymbal
S. Bells	Sleigh Bells
Tamb.	Tambourine
WB	Wood Block
Cab.	Cabasa
TB	Temple Blocks
HD	Hand Drum
BD	Bass Drum
BX	Bass Xylophone
BM	Bass Metallophone
CBB	Contrabass Bar
Timp.	Timpani (contrabass bars may be substituted as necessary)
DB	Double (String) Bass
	(contrabass bars may be substituted as necessary)

Great Big House in New Orleans

American Singing Game
arr. Matthew McCoy

2. Went down to the old mill stream,
    To fetch a pail of water.
    Put one arm around my wife,
    The other 'round my daughter.

3. Fare thee well, my darling girl,
    Fare thee well, my daughter,
    Fare thee well, my darling girl
    With the golden slippers on her.

Great Big House in New Orleans

American Singing Game

This arrangement of a classic American singing game works well for classroom use and in performance. Once the song and game have been learned, the accompaniment may be taught through the following sequence. This accompaniment may be taught through body percussion and later transferred to instruments, or each part may be taught individually and transferred immediately.

1. Teach the bass xylophone part through body percussion. For younger or inexperienced students, it may be appropriate to teach the accompaniment pattern first as quarter notes and add the rest once the beat and tempo are secure.

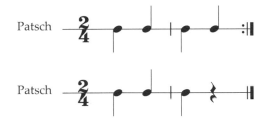

2. Teach the soprano and alto glockenspiel part by snapping on the last beat of each phrase and then transfer to barred instruments.

3. Teach the wood block part by clapping or speaking the ostinato. Once secure, transfer to percussion.

4. If desired, teach the optional introduction/interlude/coda through speech and/or body percussion. Transfer to bass xylophone (timpani or contrabass bars may also be used) and wood block.

Singing Game

Formation: Single circle of students, alternately numbered as #1 or #2

Verse 1:   All students walk or strut around the circle counter clockwise.

Verse 2:   #1s walk into the center, forming a smaller circle, during "went down to the old mill stream," and hold hands. While singing "to fetch a pail of water," #2s walk into the center, reaching inside the circle formed by the #1s. On the word "water," all #2s hold hands while still reaching inside the smaller circle. Without letting go of hands, #2s bring their arms over the heads of #1s and place them at the lower back of the #1s while singing "put one arm around my wife." During "the other 'round my daughter," #1s bring their arms over the heads of the #2s and place them at the lower back of the #2s. This movement is commonly called a daisy chain.

Verse 3:   While interlocked, students side-step to the right while singing. A variation of this movement is to ask the students to side-step with their right feet and then cross behind the right foot with the left.

Sleep, Little One

Lullaby
arr. Matthew McCoy

Sleep, lit - tle one sleep, out of doors there runs a sheep, A___

sheep with four white feet___ that___ drinks its milk so

sweet___ Sleep, lit - tle one sleep.

Sleep, Little One

Lullaby

This lullaby was collected in the United States in the first half of the 20th century and in all probability has its origin in European folk music. The arrangement is sparse, in keeping with the quiet nature of the purpose of the song, and is suitable for young and inexperienced players. The following sequence is presented with these latter students in mind.

1. Teach the bass metallophone part through body percussion performing the macro pulse as students sing the song.

    Change the body percussion to the following pattern. It may be helpful to some students to pat the outside of the leg with right hand on the second note as this mimics the playing technique of this part.

    Repeat the process on barred instruments.

2. Teach the cabasa part first by identifying specific rhyming words in the lyric (i.e., sleep, sheep, feet, and sweet). Next, use these words as cues to perform the rhythmic ostinato, first by gently clapping the rhythm and then on the cabasa.

3. Teach the finger cymbal part using the same process as the above cabasa part; however, perform with snapping in place of clapping.

4. Teach the glockenspiel part on the barred instruments if possible; otherwise, substitute body percussion, i.e., patching, performing the rhythm and then transferring to instruments at a later point. This part may be thought of as an echo to the vocal melody and it may be appropriate to begin with a simplified pattern that is then added to once the students are secure.

Simplified pattern:

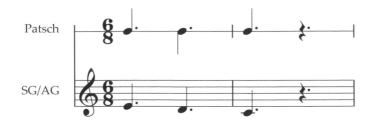

As written in the score:

Performance Considerations:

This song may be varied through the alternation of lyrics and vocables (e.g., "lu") on repetitions. Additionally, the melody may be playable by advanced recorder players who are comfortable performing F-natural on their instruments.

There Was a Pig Went Out to Dig

Traditional English Carol
arr. Matthew McCoy

2. There was a cow went out to plow...
3. There was a sparrow went out to harrow...
4. There was a crow went out to sow...
5. There was a sheep went out to reap...
6. There was a drake went out to rake...
7. There was a minnow went out to winnow...
8. Then ev'ry beast prepared the feast...
9. Let ev'ry creature on Earth now sing...

There Was a Pig Went Out to Dig

Traditional English Carol

This carol may be acted out during performance, as was the custom in years past. Once the song has been learned, the following sequence may be used to teach the accompaniment.

1. Teach the timpani and bass metallophone parts through body percussion or directly on barred instruments. Contrabass bars or bass xylophone may substitute for the timpani. The bass metallophone part may also be doubled or replaced by an alto metallophone. Perform as an accompaniment to singing.

2. Teach the soprano xylophone part first by isolating the words "was a pig went out" and clapping the melodic rhythm. Once secure, transfer to barred instruments beginning on B and descending to E.

(was   a   pig   went   out)

Perform with all verses.

3. Teach the alto and soprano glockenspiel parts through body percussion. The process is similar for both parts with minor changes added to the end. For both parts, begin with the following rhythm performed with snapping. This part is simple enough to be taught by rote in relation to the phrases of the song.

For the alto glockenspiel part, change the ending as follows. Crossing the left hand over the right for the last note may reinforce the playing technique/melodic contour.

Transfer to barred instruments once secure.

For the soprano glockenspiel part, change the ending as follows. As with the alto glockenspiel part, crossing over hands may help reinforce the playing technique/melodic contour.

Transfer to barred instruments once secure.

4. Add the triangle roll on the last note.

The recorder parts in this arrangement are optional, though if competent players are available (e.g., older students, other teachers) they add color and interest.

Charlie's Neat and Charlie's Sweet

Traditional Singing Game
arr. Matthew McCoy

2. Want no more of your weev'ly wheat,
   Want no more of your barley,
   Take some more of your good old rye
   To bake a cake for Charlie.

Chorus

3. Over the meadow we trip together,
   In the morning early,
   Heart to heart and hand to hand,
   'Tis true I love you dearly.

Chorus

4. Over and over, ten times over,
   Charlie is a rover,
   Take your partner by the hands
   And wring the dishrag over.

Chorus

Charlie's Neat and Charlie's Sweet

Traditional Singing Game

The accompaniment for this song may be taught in a variety of ways once the students have thoroughly learned the melody and lyrics. The following sequence is suggested for students who may not have experience with standard notation in the meter of 6/8.

1. Teach the bass xylophone/bass metallophone part in measures 5–12 and 13–20 through use of beat box visuals. Each box represents one beat and symbols/letters placed inside represent the sounds or notes to be performed. In this process, different body percussion levels or notes are indicated by color. The individual beat box patterns may be presented initially as flashcards or all at once. In either case, it may be appropriate to perform all Xs with one level of body percussion or a single note before using two or more levels of body percussion and/or notes.

   Verse and Chorus:

   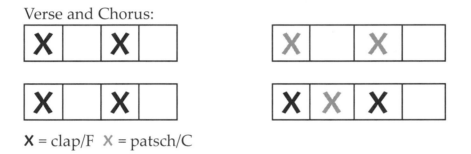

   X = clap/F   X = patsch/C

2. Teach the alto xylophone part through beat box visuals performed by patsching or playing the note C on barred instruments.

   Verse (measures 5–12):

   Chorus, simplified pattern (measures 13–20):

   Chorus as written in score (measures 13–20):

3. Teach the soprano glockenspiel accompaniment pattern for measures 13–20.

   Chorus

   X = patsch/C   X = clap/high C

Once the rhythm and notes are secure, add the glissando as notated in the score.

4. Add the remaining accompaniment patterns through use of beat box visuals, speech, or by rote imitation. Transfer to the indicated instruments once each part has been learned.

Performance considerations:
The introduction to this arrangement may also be performed on other treble instruments (e.g., flute or violin).

This singing game is an excellent vehicle that can provide an opportunity for students to create choreographies in folk-dance style. An example follows.

Formation: Longways Set

<u>Section</u>	<u>Movement</u>
Verse 1	Top couple sashays down and back up the set
Chorus	All forward and back Do-si-do partner
Verse 2	Right hand turn Left hand turn
Chorus	(as before)
Verse 3	Right hand star (with an adjacent couple) Left hand star
Chorus	(as before)
Verse 4 & Chorus	Cast off and thread the needle

'Liza Jane

2. I've got a house in Baltimore, Lil' Liza Jane,
   Street car runs right by my door, Lil' Liza Jane.

3. I've got a house in Baltimore, Lil' Liza Jane,
   Brussels carpet on my floor, Lil' Liza Jane.

4. I've got a house in Baltimore, Lil' Liza Jane.
   Silver doorplate on the door, Lil' Liza Jane.

'Liza Jane

American Folk Song

The accompaniment for this song may be taught in a variety of ways once the students have securely learned the melody and lyrics. The following teaching suggestions use speech and body percussion as preparations for various parts of the accompaniment.

1. Prepare the non-pitched percussion parts in measures 9–16 through the following speech ostinati.

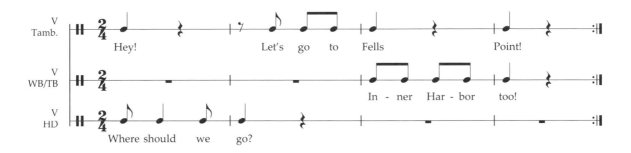

N.B.: Fells Point and Inner Harbor are two favorite destinations for people visiting the downtown area of Baltimore.

Once secure, the speech ostinati should be used to accompany singing and then transferred to tambourine, wood block, and hand drum.

2. Teach the bass xylophone part for measures 1–8 and measures 9–16 through use of beat box visuals. Each box represents one beat and symbols/letters placed inside represent the sounds or notes to be performed. In this process, different body percussion levels or notes are indicated by color. The individual beat box patterns may be presented initially as flashcards or all at once. In either case, it may be appropriate to perform the Xs with one level of body percussion or a single note before using two or more levels of body percussion and/or notes. Additionally, while the meter of this piece is 2/4, the beat boxes have been grouped in fours to assist with pattern recognition and retention.

(measures 1–8 and 9–16)

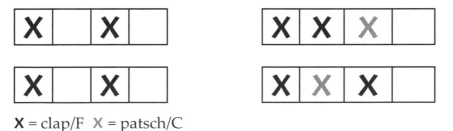

X = clap/F X = patsch/C

Once students are secure and can perform this part as an accompaniment to singing, the additional notes in measures 4 and 12 may be added.

2. Prepare the alto xylophone part in measures 1–8 through the following body percussion sequence, practicing each until secure before proceeding to the next.

Once secure, transfer to barred instruments.

3. Prepare the alto xylophone part in measures 9–16 through the following body percussion sequence taught by rote or with standard notation, practicing each until secure before proceeding to the next.

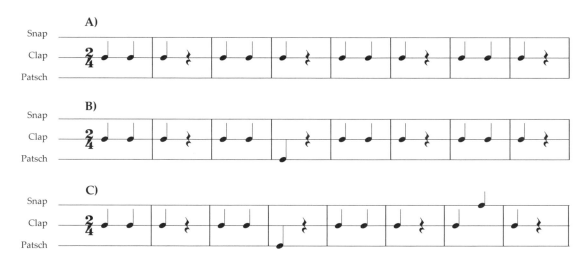

Once secure, transfer to barred instruments using the following sequence, practicing each until secure before proceeding to the next.

4. Prepare the soprano glockenspiel part by snapping on the final beat of each phrase and transfer to barred instruments.

5. Teach the soprano xylophone part in measures 9–16 by first clapping the rhythm while singing. Once secure, transfer to the barred instruments using the following sequence, practicing each until secure before proceeding to the next.

Performance considerations:
This folk game is an excellent vehicle that can provide an opportunity for students to create choreographies in folk-dance style. An example of a dance is provided in the performance considerations for *Charlie's Neat and Charlie's Sweet*.

Welcome Here

American Shaker
arr. Matthew McCoy

Wel-come here,   wel-come here,   All be a-live and be

of good cheer! Wel-come here,   wel-come here,   All be a-live and be of good cheer!

2. I've got a log that's burning hot
   Coffee's bubbling in the pot.
   Come in, ye people, where it's warm,
   The wind blows sharp and it may storm.

3. I made a loaf that's cooling there,
   With my neighbors I will share.
   Come, all ye people, hear me sing
   A song of friendly welcoming.

Welcome Here

American Shaker

The accompaniment for this song may be taught in a variety of ways once the students have securely learned the melody and lyrics. The following is one suggested sequence appropriate for older students.

1. Teach the bass xylophone/bass metallophone part for measures 3–18 through body percussion (i.e., movement imitating playing technique) or by rote on the barred instruments. For the latter it may be appropriate to sing the entire song performing only the refrain accompaniment and again using the accompaniment for the verses. After both have been introduced, simply change the accompaniment patterns according to the form of the song.

2. Teach the soprano xylophone and soprano glockenspiel parts for measures 11–18 together by rote or with standard notation. Once learned, divide the parts between instruments and perform while singing.

Unison:

Divided:

3. Add the sleigh bells to the accompaniment of all verses (measures 11–18).

4. Teach the alto xylophone part for measures 3–10 through body percussion. It is recommended that students attend to where hands alternate.

Once secure, transfer to barred instruments first performing on C:

And then on C and D:

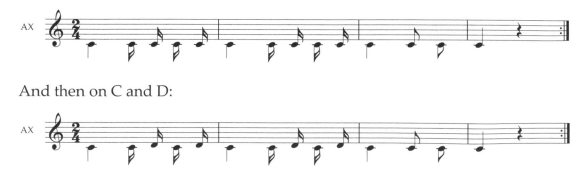

5. Teach the timpani part through body percussion and then transfer to barred instruments and timpani (or contrabass bars if no timpani are available).

6. Teach the temple blocks part through body percussion then transfer to percussion. The following sequence may be appropriate when introducing this accompaniment pattern to a group of students.

   Begin with a simplified body percussion pattern:

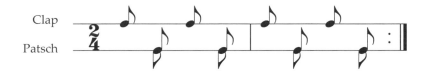

   Change the second measure of the pattern (alternating hands when patsching):

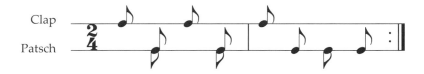

   Transfer to temple blocks, substituting stick clicks for each clap and performing the patches on the instrument:

   In effect, this will produce the offbeat pattern written in the score. Once secure, the stick click may be performed quietly or eliminated entirely.

Orchestration Consideration:
The introduction is written for soprano recorder, though it is also suitable for other treble instruments (e.g., flute, violin, or glockenspiel).

Father Grumble

American Folk Song
arr. Matthew McCoy

2. "But you must milk the tiny cow
   For fear she should go dry,
   And you must feed the little pigs
   That are within the sty.
   And you must watch the bracket hen
   Lest she lay astray,
   And you must wind the reel of yarn
   That I spun yesterday."

3. The old woman took the staff in her hand
   And went to drive the plow;
   The old man took the pail in his hand
   And went to milk the cow;
   But Tiny hinched and Tiny flinched
   And Tiny cocked her nose
   And Tiny gave the old man such a kick
   That the blood ran down to his toes.

4. 'T'was, "Hey my good cow," and
   "How my good cow,"
   And "Now my good cow, stand still.
   If ever I milk this cow again,
   'Twill be against my will."
   And when he'd milked the tiny cow
   For fear she should go dry,
   Why, then he fed the little pigs
   That were within the sty.

5. And then he watched the bracket hen,
   Lest she should lay astray,
   But he forgot the reel of yarn
   His wife spun yesterday.
   He swore by all the leaves on the tree,
   And all the stars in heaven,
   That his wife could do more work in a day
   Than he could do in seven.

Father Grumble

American Folk Song

Once this song has been learned the majority of the accompaniment may be taught through body percussion and then transferred to barred instruments and non-pitched percussion.

1. Teach the soprano xylophone and timpani parts for measures 5–20 together with the following body percussion. Repeat the pattern four times as an accompaniment to singing.

    Once secure, change the accompaniment in the third phrase (measures 13–16) as follows:

    Perform again with the change in the third phrase as an accompaniment to singing.

2. Teach the bass xylophone part for measures 5–20 by patching the following pattern. Repeat four times as an accompaniment to singing.

    Once secure, change the accompaniment in the third phrase (measures 13–16) as follows:

    Perform again as an accompaniment to singing.

3. The soprano/alto glockenspiel part in measures 5–20 may be taught using the same process in the previous two steps. Begin with the following pattern performed with snapping.

    Once secure, change the accompaniment in the third phrase (measures 13–16) as follows:

Change the accompaniment for the third phrase again.

Snap

Perform as an accompaniment to singing.

4. Teach the wood block part in measures 5–20 by clapping the rhythm at the end of each phrase.

(Repeat 4 times)

Clap

5. Transfer all parts to barred instruments and non-pitched percussion.

6. Teach the introduction through body percussion, with a text, or rote imitation.

The Piper o' Dundee

Scottish Folk Song
arr. Matthew McCoy

Verse 2 (4 in the original):

It's some gat swords, and some gat nane,
And some were dancin' mad their lane,
And mony a vow o' weir was ta'en,
That nicht at Amulrie.

The Piper o' Dundee

Scottish Folk Song

1. Teach the following melodic motive on the barred instruments or by clapping the melodic rhythm. Once secure, add the mallet click at the end of the melodic pattern (to be later transferred to non-pitched percussion).

Identify where in the song this melodic motive occurs (at the end of each section) and perform as appropriate. Replace the mallet clicks with a glissando in the soprano glockenspiel.

2. Teach the bass xylophone/bass metallophone part for measures 3–6 and 11–14 through the following body percussion. Once secure, transfer to barred instruments replacing patching with G and D and clapping with the previously learned melodic motive (from step 1). Once students are able to sing and accompany the melody, shift the accompaniment to F and C in measures 4 and 12.

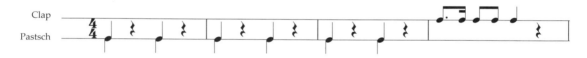

The bass metallophone part is easily taught once the bass xylophone part has been learned.

3. Teach the bass xylophone part for measures 7–10 on the barred instruments, first as half notes and then as quarter notes, substituting the motive from step 1 in measure 10.

4. Teach the soprano xylophone part for measures 7–10 on the barred instruments, first as half notes and then with the notated rhythm. Note that this part ends with the descending melodic motive learned in step 1.

5. Teach the soprano glockenspiel part for measures 3–6 and 11–14 using the following body percussion. Once secure, transfer to barred instruments first on G and high G and then adding the F and high F as notated.

(x = mallet click)

6. Add the non-pitched percussion parts taught by rote or with notation.

Performance Considerations

The soprano recorder obbligato in measures 11–14 is optional, though if competent players are available (e.g., older students, other teachers) it adds color and interest. Further, this part may also be performed on flute or fiddle.

Notes on Lyrics

As provided by Doreen Falby, director of the Peabody Children's Chorus

The verses in this arrangement were selected according to their ease of singing. The other verses, many of which may be found via the internet, mention all the tunes the Piper played. The point of the song is that the Piper o' Dundee kept playing tune after tune and no one could stand still. Hence, he was a "rogie" (i.e., rogue) and behaved in a manner that was disapproved of, yet added to his likability and charm.

The piper *cam' tae oor toun,*   came to our town
Tae oor toon, tae oor toun
The piper cam' tae oor toun
And he play'd *bonnielie*   [pron. bonnily] prettily, well
He play'd a *spring* the *laird* to please   lively dance; land owner
A spring *brent* new *frae yont* the seas   sprung forth; from beyond
And then he *gi'ed* his bags a squeeze   gave
And played *anither* key   another

Chorus:

And *wasna he a rougie*, a rougie, a rougie,   wasn't he a rogue
And wasna he a rougie, the piper o' Dundee

The piper cam' tae oor toun,
Tae oor toon, tae oor toun
The piper cam' tae oor toun
And he play'd bonnielie
It's *some gat swords* and some gat nane   some were sword dancing
And some were dancin' mad *their lane*   alone
And *mony a vow o' weir was ta'en*   many a vow of war was taken
That *nicht* at Amulrie.   night; town in Scotland

The Blooming Bright Star of Belle Isle

Newfoundland Folk Song
arr. Matthew McCoy

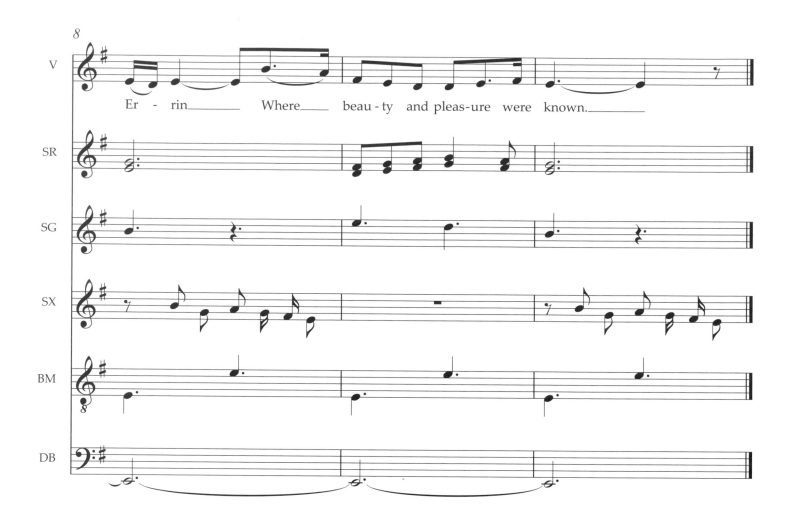

2. I spied a fair maid at her labor,
   Which caused me to stay for a while;
   I thought her the goddess of beauty,
   The Blooming Bright Star of Belle Isle.

3. "I own you're the maid I love dearly;
   You've been on my heart all the while.
   For me there is no other damsel
   Than my Blooming Bright Star of Belle Isle."

The Blooming Bright Star of Belle Isle

Newfoundland Folk Song

Once the song has been learned, the accompaniment may be taught in the following sequence.

1. Teach the bass metallophone part to establish the beat and an appropriate tempo.

2. Teach the soprano glockenspiel part through mirror imitation. Once secure, transfer to barred instruments.

3. Teach the soprano xylophone part by first patching the melodic rhythm as a response to the soprano glockenspiel accompaniment.

   Once students are secure with alternating hands while performing the melodic rhythm, teach the accompaniment pattern through the following note sequence on barred instruments, practicing each until secure before proceeding to the next.

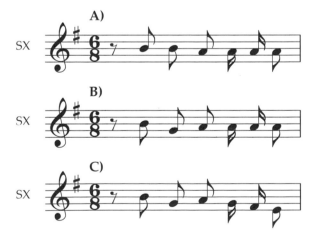

4. Teach the recorder parts by presenting the following visual and asking students to review the notes from D to high D (including F♯s). Provide opportunity to practice playing up and down the pitch set.

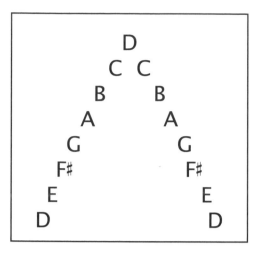

Repeat the previous process, this time eliminating the C from the pitch set.

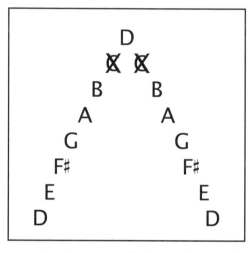

Once students are secure playing up and down the pitch set, present the following melodic configuration. Ask the students to perform the motive beginning on any note in the pitch set (with the omitted Cs). Provide opportunity to practice, share, and discuss the possibilities.

Next, ask the students to perform the melodic configuration beginning on an E and perform four times. Once secure, change the fourth repetition by shifting the motive down one note. Begin this pattern on D.

Play the motive three times beginning on E followed by the motive beginning on D once.

Change the motive beginning on D by abbreviating the motive and ending on E. Once secure, teach the rhythm of this final motive by rote.

The Tailor and the Mouse

English Folk Song
arr. Matthew McCoy

2. The tailor had a tall silk hat, Hi diddle umkum feedle.
   The mouse, he ate it, fancy that, Hi diddle umkum feedle.

3. The tailor thought the mouse was ill, Hi diddle umkum feedle.
   He gave him part of a big blue pill, Hi diddle umkum feedle.

4. The tailor thought his mouse would die, Hi diddle umkum feedle.
   He baked him in an apple pie, Hi diddle umkum feedle.

5. The pie was cut, the mouse ran out, Hi diddle umkum feedle.
   The tailor followed him all about, Hi diddle umkum feedle.

6. The tailor chased him over the lea, Hi diddle umkum feedle.
   The last of that mouse he never did see, Hi diddle umkum feedle.

The Tailor and the Mouse

English Folk Song

The accompaniment for this song may be taught in a variety of ways once the students have thoroughly learned the melody and lyrics. The following sequence is suggested for students who may not have many experiences with elemental accompaniments that incorporate chord changes.

1. Teach the bass xylophone and timpani parts for measures 5–20 through cooperative work between partners or small groups. The following is one option for preparing the accompaniment through movement and hand game possibilities.

    First, teach the following hand game activity.

    Perform as an accompaniment for the entire song. Once secure, change the third phrase accompaniment in measures 13–16 as follows.

    Perform entire hand game as an accompaniment to singing. Once secure, transfer to barred instruments performing the bass xylophone accompaniment. To transfer to the timpani, add the sixteenth note rhythm to phrases 1, 2, and 4 and tacet on phrase 3.

2. Teach the alto xylophone part in measures 5–20 through body percussion and immediately transfer to barred instruments.

    First, teach the following rhythm to be performed with patching.

    Perform as an accompaniment for the entire song. Once secure, change the third phrase accompaniment in measures 13–16 as follows.

    Perform again as an accompaniment to singing.

3. Present the following simplified staff visual and teach the soprano xylophone accompaniment in measures 5–20 on the barred instruments. Ask the students to perform this melodic pattern beginning on A.

Perform the simplified melodic pattern in half notes as an accompaniment to phrases 1, 2, and 4. Once secure, add the following sequence of changes/ additions, practicing each until secure before proceeding to the next.

A)

SX

B)

SX

C)

SX

D)

SX

Again, perform the final sequence as an accompaniment to phrases 1, 2, and 4. Once secure, ask the students to perform the same melodic pattern beginning on high C. Ask the student to perform either pattern or both simultaneously. Perform again as accompaniment.

4. The soprano glockenspiel part in measures 5–20 may be taught directly on the barred instruments using a melodic skeleton. Depending on the experience level of the students, a notated example may be appropriate to use in the following sequence; otherwise, this may also be taught by rote.

The initial melodic skeleton:

SG

Suggested sequence of additions/changes:

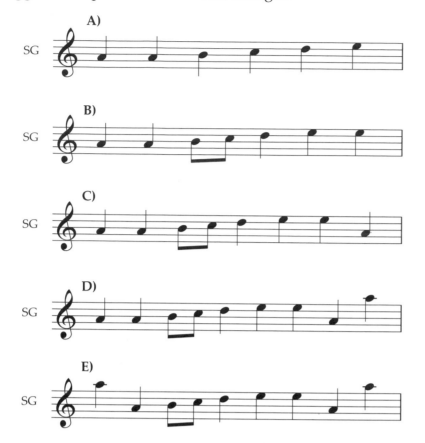

Once secure, the glissando may be added to the end. Perform the final sequence as an accompaniment to phrases 1, 2, and 4.

Phrase 3 (measures 13–16) may be taught through scalar patterns beginning with A to high A, then shifted one step lower, i.e. G to high G. Alternation of hands is recommended. Once patterns have been learned, add the eighth note rhythm and perform in context with the remaining accompaniment.

Orff-Schulwerk American Edition

MAIN VOLUMES

Music for Children 1	Pre-School	SMC 12
Music for Children 2	Primary	SMC 6
Music for Children 3	Upper Elementary	SMC 8

SUPPLEMENTARY PUBLICATIONS

AFRICAN SONGS FOR SCHOOL AND COMMUNITY
(Robert Kwami) SMC 551
A selection of 12 songs including traditional material and original compositions by the author.

THE ANCIENT FACE OF NIGHT (Gerald Dyck) SMC 553
A collection of original songs and instrumental pieces for SATB chorus and Orff instruments. The cycle of songs has both astronomical and musical influences. (Chorus Part: SMC 553-01)

ANIMAL CRACKER SUITE AND OTHER POEMS
(Deborah A. Imiolo-Schriver) SMC 561
A set of four original poems arranged for speech chorus, body percussion and percussion ensemble. Twenty-one additional original poems are included for teachers and students to make their own musical settings.

ALL AROUND THE BUTTERCUP (Ruth Boshkoff) SMC 24
These folk song arrangements are organized progressively, each new note being introduced separately.

CHIPMUNKS, CICADAS AND OWLS (Natalie Sarrazin) SMC 552
Twelve native American children's songs from different regions.

CIRCUS RONDO (Donald Slagel) SMC 73
A stylized circus presentation using music, movement, speech and improvisational technique, for various Orff instruments, recorders and voices.

CROCODILE AND OTHER POEMS (Ruth Pollock Hamm) SMC 15
A collection of verses for use as choral speech within the elementary school. Included are ideas for movement, instrumental accompaniments, and proposals for related art, drama and listening activities.

DANCING SONGS (Phillip Rhodes) SMC 35
A song cycle for voices and Orff instruments. The contemporary harmonies create a dramatic and sophisticated experience for upper elementary/middle school grades.

DE COLORES (Virginia Ebinger) SMC 20
Folklore from the Hispanic tradition for voices, recorders and classroom percussion.

DISCOVERING KEETMAN (Jane Frazee) SMC 547
Rhythmic exercises and pieces for xylophone by Gunild Keetman. Selected and introduced by Jane Frazee.

DOCUM DAY (Donald Slagel) SMC 18
An olio of songs from England, Hungary, Ireland, Jamaica, the Middle East, Newfoundland, Nova Scotia, the USA. For voices, recorders and classroom percussion.

EIGHT MINIATURES (Hermann Regner) SMC 14
Ensemble pieces for advanced players of recorders and Orff instruments which lead directly from elementary 'Music for Children'; to chamber music for recorders.

ELEMENTAL RECORDER PLAYING
(Gunild Keetman and Minna Ronnefeld) Translation by Mary Shamrock
Teacher's Book SMC 558
This book is based on the fundamental principles of Orff-Schulwerk. The book can be used as a foundation text in an elementary music program that includes use of the recorder. It can also be employed in teaching situations that concentrate primarily upon recorder but in which ensemble playing, improvisation and singing also play an essential role.
Student's Book SMC 559
Includes a variety of exercises, songs, pieces, improvisation exercises, canons, duets, rondos and texts to use for making rhythms and melodies.
Student's Workbook SMC 560
Contains exercises and games for doing at home and during the music lesson. Integrated with work in the Student's Book.

FENCE POSTS AND OTHER POEMS (Ruth Pollock Hamm) SMC 31
Texts for melodies, 'Sound Envelopes', movement and composition written by children, selected poets and the editor. Material for creative melody making and improvisation (including jazz).

FOUR PSALM SETTINGS (Sue Ellen Page) SMC 30
For treble voices (unison and two-part) and Orff instruments.

HAVE YOU ANY WOOL? THREE BAGS FULL! (Richard Gill) SMC 29
17 traditional rhymes for voices and Orff instruments. Speech exercises, elaborate settings for Orff instruments using nursery rhymes to show how to play with texts.

HELLO CHILDREN (Shirley Salmon) SMC 572
A collection of songs and related activities for children aged 4–9

KUKURÍKU (Miriam Samuelson) SMC 57
Traditional Hebrew songs and dances (including Hava Nagila) arranged for voices, recorders and Orff instruments. Instructions (with diagrams) are given for the dances.

THE MAGIC FOREST (Lynn Johnson) SMC 16
Sequenced, early childhood, music-lesson plans based on the Orff-Schulwerk approach.

PIECES AND PROCESSES (Steven Calantropio) SMC 569
This collection of original songs, exercises, instrumental pieces, and arrangements provides fresh examples of elemental music. Along with each piece is a detailed teaching procedure designed to give music educators a collection of instructional techniques.

THE QUANGLE WANGLE'S HAT (Sara Newberry) SMC 32
Edward Lear's delightful poem set for speaker(s), recorders and Orff instruments (with movement and dance improvisation).

¡QUIEN CANTA SU MAL ESPANTA!
Songs, Games and Dances from Latin America
(Sofia Lopez-Ibor and Verena Maschat) SMC 568
This book presents a rich and varied selection of material from an immense geographical area, combining local traditions with foreign influences to engage and inspire teachers and students. The DVD includes demonstrations of the dances for presentation in the classroom.

THE RACCOON PHILOSOPHER
(Danai Gagne-Apostolidou and Judith Thomas-Solomon) SMC 566
A drama in mixed meters for upper elementary grades with preparatory activities for singing, moving, playing recorder, Orff instruments and creating. The Raccoon Philosopher was inspired by thoughts on virtue by Martin Buber. As we learn from the raccoon, so we learn from the children: to be merry for no particular reason, to never for a moment be idle, and to express our needs vigorously.

RECORDERS WITH ORFF ENSEMBLE (Isabel McNeill Carley) SMC 25-27
Three books designed to fill a need for a repertoire (pentatonic and diatonic) for beginning and intermediate recorder players. Most of the pieces are intended to be both played and danced and simple accompaniments are provided.

RINGAROUND, SINGAROUND (Ruth Boshkoff) SMC 33
Games, rhymes and folksongs for the early elementary grades, arranged in sequential order according to concepts.

ROUND THE CORNER AND AWAY WE GO (David J. Gonzol) SMC 567
This folk song collection provides models of arrangements to be taught using Orff-Schulwerk processes. The accompanying teaching suggestions give examples of how to break down instrumental parts and sequence the presentation of them developmentally.

RRRRRO
(Polyxene Mathéy and Angelika Panagopoulos-Slavik) SMC 79
Poetry, music and dance from Greece with Greek texts adapted for rhythmic reciting by groups accompanied by percussion and other instruments.

A SEASONAL KALEIDOSCOPE
(Joyce Coffey, Danai Gagne, Laura Koulish) SMC 55
Original songs, poetry and stories with Orff instruments for children. Bound by a theme of seasonal changes and intended for classroom and music teachers.

SIMPLY SUNG (Mary Goetze) SMC 23
Folk songs arranged in three parts for young singers. They include American folk songs, spirituals and Hebrew melodies.

SKETCHES IN STYLE (Carol Richards and Neil Aubrey) SMC 19
Arrangements for classroom music. For voices, recorders and classroom percussion.

SOMETHING TOLD THE WILD GEESE (Craig Earley) SMC 21
A collection of folksongs for unison treble voices, barred and small percussion instruments, and recorders (soprano and alto).

STREET GAMES (Gloria Fuoco-Lawson) SMC 17
Instrumental arrangements of rhythmical hand jives based on traditional American street games.

TALES TO TELL, TALES TO PLAY
(Carol Erion and Linda Monssen) SMC 28
Four folk tales (Indian, African, German and American Indian) retold and arranged for music and movement, with accompaniment for recorders and Orff instruments.

TEN FOLK CAROLS FOR CHRISTMAS FROM THE UNITED STATES
(Jane Frazee) SMC 22
Settings of Appalachian and unfamiliar carols, arranged for voices, recorders and Orff instruments.

TUNES FOR YOUNG TROUBADOURS (Dianne Ladendecker) SMC 34
Ten songs for children's voices, recorders and Orff ensemble.

WIND SONGS (Phillip Rhodes) SMC 197
Four songs for unison voices, barred and small percussion instruments.

ORFF SCHULWERK PUBLICATIONS

Playing Together
An Introduction to Teaching Orff-Instrument Skills by Jane Frazee
49017079 . . . .$14.95

¡Quien canta su mal espanta! (Singing Drives Away Sorrow)
Songs, Games and Dances from Latin America by Sophia Lopez-Ibor and Verena Maschat
49015641   Book/DVD pack $29.95

Pieces and Processes
by Steven Calantropio
This collection of original songs, exercises, instrumental pieces and arrangements of traditional material provides fresh examples of elemental music in a wide variety of styles. Detailed teaching procedures provide a 'Process Teaching Toolbox', organized by musical element.
49013585 . . . .$17.95

Play, Sing, & Dance
An Introduction to Orff Schulwerk by Doug Goodkin
An overview of the dynamic approach to music education known as Orff Schulwerk. In this comprehensive look at the many facets of this timeless practice, Doug Goodkin re-imagines its import in the lives of children, schools and culture at large in contemporary times.
49012187 . . . .$26.95

Orff Schulwerk Today
Nurturing Musical Expression and Understanding by Jane Frazee
This book is addressed to all music teachers who want to develop clarity of purpose in a child-centred educational environment. It presents a fresh synthesis of doing and understanding that encourages students to express themselves in—and realize themselves through—music.
49012187 Book/CD pack $54.95

Discovering Orff
A Curriculum for Music Teachers by Jane Frazee with Kent Kreuter
This book is intended for those who want detailed, practical assistance in how and why to use Orff techniques and materials in the classroom.
49012199 . . . .$39.95

Exploring Orff
A Teacher's Guide by Arvida Steen
Practical advice on how to form an appropriate curriculum, choose the best materials and plan lessons that have a clear focus and are also open to frequent student contributions.
49012193 . . . .$49.95

Gunild Keetman
A Life for Movement and Music by Minne Lange-Ronnefeld & Hermann Regner
Gunild Keetman (1904–1990) was co-author of the Orff Schulwerk. Making use of texts, photos and extensive documentary material, the present volume vividly describes the life of this artist and pedagogue. The accompanying DVD includes interesting audio documents and film excerpts.
49008492 Book/DVD pack. $49.95

Discovering Keetman
(Gunild Keetman)
Rhythmic exercises and pieces for xylophone, selected and introduced by Jane Frazee.
49012172 . . . .$22.95